THE YOUNG PERSON'S GUIDE TO THE

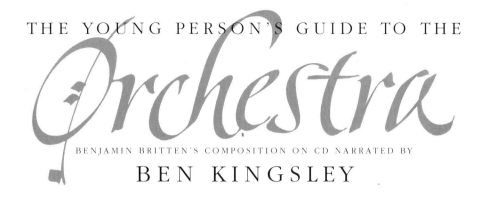

Orchestra

BENJAMIN BRITTEN'S COMPOSITION ON CD NARRATED BY

BEN KINGSLEY

THE YOUNG PERSON'S GUIDE TO THE

Orchestra

BENJAMIN BRITTEN'S COMPOSITION ON CD NARRATED BY

BEN KINGSLEY

BOOK WRITTEN BY

ANITA GANERI

HARCOURT BRACE & COMPANY

SAN DIEGO   NEW YORK   LONDON

First published in Great Britain in 1996 by
PAVILION BOOKS LIMITED
2 6 Upper Ground, London SE1 9PD

First U.S. edition 1996

Library of Congress Cataloging-in-Publication Data
Ganeri, Anita, 1961–
The young person's guide to the orchestra: Benjamin Britten's
composition on CD/narrated by Ben Kingsley.
p. cm.
Includes index.
Summary: Provides information about the history of
the orchestra since its beginnings in the seventeenth century,
instruments of the orchestra, and famous composers of classical music.
ISBN 0-15-201304-0
1. Orchestra—Juvenile literature. 2. Music appreciation—Juvenile literature.
[1. Orchestra. 2. Musical instruments. 3. Music appreciation.]
I. Britten, Benjamin, 1913–1976. Young person's guide to the orchestra.
II. Title.
ML3928.G36 1996 <Phon Case>
784.2—dc20 95-41478

A B C D E

Printed in China

Contents

Introduction

elcome to the sights and sounds of the orchestra! What makes classical music so wonderfully expressive is the great range of instruments. Each instrument has an individual sound that can play a gentle melody, a dramatic, majestic tune, or the rhythm that shapes the music.

Benjamin Britten wrote this music and narration (included on the CD at the front of this book) to bring the excitement of orchestral music to a wider audience. After being introduced to the sounds of each instrument—from mellow flutes to blazing trumpets—you will discover much more about the orchestra and its instruments. When did the first orchestras exist? Who were the great classical composers? How does a woodwind instrument produce sound? Where do the four instrumental sections sit in a modern symphony orchestra? You will find the answers to these questions, and many more, on the following pages.

What Is an Orchestra?

The concert hall buzzes with voices as the audience takes their seats. Snatches of music rise from the orchestra as musicians tune their instruments. When the conductor steps on stage silence falls.

What is an orchestra?

An orchestra is a large group of musicians with instruments that play the classical music of Europe, Russia, and North America. The orchestra plays music written by a composer to make use of all the different instruments and their various sounds. When all the instruments play together, the music blends into one magnificent sound.

DID YOU KNOW?

The word *orchestra* was first used by the ancient Greeks over 2,000 years ago. It did not have the same meaning as it does today. It was the name for the dance floor in front of the stage in the Greek theater where the actors sang and danced during a play.

On June 17, 1872, in Boston, Massachusetts, Johann Strauss the Younger conducted the largest orchestra ever to play. It was made up of 987 instruments, including 400 first violins, and was accompanied by a choir of 20,000 singers.

The London Symphony Orchestra

Who's who in an orchestra?

he modern orchestra may contain more than 100 instruments, divided into four sections, or families: string, brass, percussion, and woodwind.

The string section contains violins, violas, cellos, and double basses.

The conductor in charge

ith so many instruments and musicians, the conductor's role is essential. He or she stands facing the orchestra, beating time with a baton and making sure that the orchestra stays in time, in tune, and that the different instruments start and stop playing at the right times. A good conductor controls the sound of the whole orchestra. His or her interpretation of the music brings out the excitement, drama, or gentleness of the composition and makes it all the more enjoyable for the listener.

Herbert von Karajan

The brass section contains French horns, trumpets, trombones, and tubas.

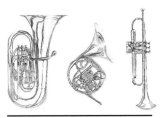

The percussion section contains drums, cymbals, gongs, triangles, xylophones, and tambourines.

The woodwind section contains clarinets, oboes, flutes, and bassoons.

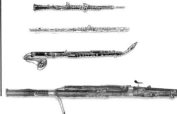

How Orchestras Began

The first orchestras existed about 400 years ago, but they were very different from today's orchestra. They were smaller, looser in structure, and comprised a narrower range of instruments.

Early orchestras

The earliest orchestras were simply groups of musicians, large or small, playing together on whatever instruments they had at hand. These were mainly string instruments, such as violins, violas, and cellos. No fixed rules stated which instruments should comprise an orchestra or how they should be organized. In the picture below, one of the women is playing an early string instrument called a lute. It is the oldest ancestor of the violin.

MONTEVERDI

In 1607, the Italian composer Claudio Monteverdi (1567–1643) used an orchestra of forty instruments to accompany his first opera, *Orfeo*. The orchestra included fifteen viols, two violins, flutes, early oboes, trumpets, trombones, two harpsichords, two organs, and a harp. These were probably the most readily available instruments at the time and not a deliberate collection.

A sixteenth-century concert

Musical movements

Classical compositions are divided into different periods, depending on the date and style of the music.

- **Baroque**—the baroque movement lasted from 1600–1750. It took its name from the grand, ornate style of architecture popular at the time. Famous baroque composers included Bach and Handel.
- **Classical**—the classical movement lasted from about 1750–1825. In music as well as architecture, it described a style that was more graceful than the baroque style. Mozart and Haydn were famous classical composers.
- **Romantic**—the nineteenth century saw the rise of the romantic movement. Music became more expressive and emotional than ever before. Romantic composers included Beethoven and Liszt.
- **Twentieth Century**—composers in Europe and America experimented with different kinds of orchestras and new "modern" sounds. Stravinsky and Mahler were twentieth-century composers.

Changing instruments

In the seventeenth and eighteenth centuries, the variety and mix of instruments used in an orchestra changed as instrument design was improved and new instruments were invented. Early in the seventeenth century, violins replaced viols to bring a brighter, richer sound to the music. They remain the most important string instruments today.

Viol

Violin

The Golden Age

The nineteenth century was the orchestra's golden age. The range of instruments was far greater than ever before, and orchestras grew bigger and bigger.

From court to concert hall

Early orchestras were employed by the king or other members of the nobility to play at court or at private gatherings. When opera and ballet became popular in the seventeenth century, orchestras were solicited to accompany the singers and dancers. By the nineteenth century, new orchestras and auditoriums built especially for use as concert halls sprang up in Europe and the United States. The public could now pay to hear the world's finest musicians.

CHANGE OF TUNE

Composers in the nineteenth century began to write music specifically for orchestras, with different parts for different instruments. As the music became more technically demanding, the orchestra grew. With a broader range of instruments, more complex music could be written. The most important new musical form was called the symphony. This was a long work, broken into several sections called movements, designed to contrast and balance the various instruments (see p. 33).

An eighteenth-century concert given to celebrate the marriage of Louis XVI

Orchestras in the twentieth century

 y the early twentieth century, some orchestras had grown very large indeed, with more than 100 musicians and possibly a choir as well. Composers such as Gustav Mahler (1860–1911) and Richard Strauss (1864–1949) wrote grand, dramatic works for them to play. Today's composers tend to write for much smaller groups or for different combinations of instruments. Modern symphony orchestras mainly play music written in the classical or romantic periods.

DID YOU KNOW?

 The German composer Richard Wagner (1813–1883) wrote a series of grand operas that required very large orchestras to accompany them. He built his own opera house in Bayreuth, Germany, where the orchestra was hidden from the audience so that it did not distract their attention from the action on stage.

In Mozart's time (1756–1791), an orchestra might consist of about thirty-five musicians. In the early nineteenth century, Beethoven wrote for an orchestra of sixty. But by the late nineteenth century, orchestras were over 100 strong, including fifty to sixty string instruments.

The Royal Festival Hall, London

Take Your Seats

A modern orchestra is a carefully organized group of musicians, their instruments, and their conductor. The string, woodwind, brass, and percussion sections each have their own special place in the orchestra and a unique part to play.

Seating plan

In a large orchestra, the musicians are arranged in a semicircle facing the conductor and the audience. The different families of instruments are grouped together, with the loudest at the back and the quietest at the front. The principal violinist has the task of leading the other musicians.

The Royal Philharmonic Orchestra

BEATS TO THE BAR

The conductor uses a small stick, called a baton, to beat time. He usually holds the baton in his right hand. He uses his left hand to indicate how the music should be interpreted—loudly or softly, briskly or flowingly. Many conductors are dramatic performers in their own right.

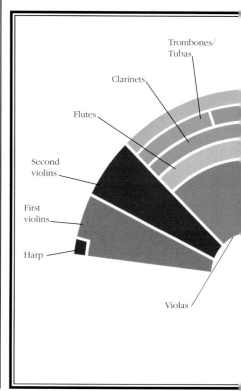

Trombones/Tubas

Clarinets

Flutes

Second violins

First violins

Harp

Violas

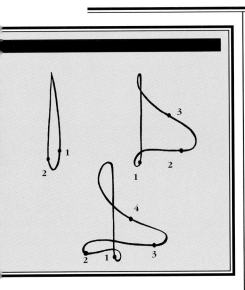

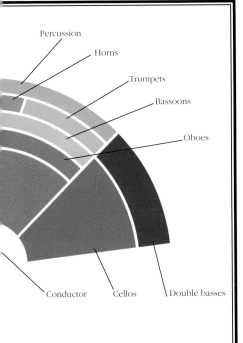

Percussion

Horns

Trumpets

Bassoons

Oboes

Conductor   Cellos   Double basses

Tuning up

All the instruments in an orchestra must play at the same pitch, otherwise they will sound out of tune. Heat and moisture can quickly cause an instrument to go out of tune, but the oboe is less affected than most. So, just before a concert begins, the oboe plays the note Middle A to which all the other instruments tune up.

Watch the conductor

Until the nineteenth century, orchestras were small enough to be directed by a violinist or from the harpsichord. However, as they got larger and the music became more complicated, a conductor was needed to keep the musicians playing together and in time. One of the first people to specialize in conducting was the German Hans Richter in 1876, but many composers, such as Wagner and Berlioz, conducted their own music. Today, every orchestra has its own conductor. He or she studies the music closely and decides exactly how it should be played before rehearsing it with the orchestra and directing the performance.

DID YOU KNOW?

The French composer Jean-Baptiste Lully (1632–1687) conducted his own works by beating time on the floor with a heavy wooden staff . . . with terrible consequences. While conducting one evening, he missed the floor and crushed his toe instead. He died of gangrene shortly thereafter.

The conductor Sir Colin Davis rehearsing with musicans

The String Section

In most modern orchestras, the string section is the largest group of instruments. It is made up of first and second violins, violas, cellos, and double basses.

Bring on the strings

The string section consists of instruments that all look very similar, except in size, and are played in the same way. They provide a rich, powerful body of sound in the orchestra, and are also used in solo pieces. The first violins appeared in about 1550 in Italy. They replaced another group of stringed instruments called viols. These had six strings and were played resting between the knees. A violin has four strings and is played resting under the chin. The string instruments are placed in front of the orchestra, from left to right. Many famous pieces of classical music have been written for string quartets—consisting of two violins, a viola, and a cello. This kind of music is called chamber music (see p. 32) because it can be performed in a room, or chamber, rather than a concert hall.

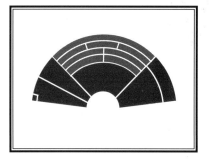

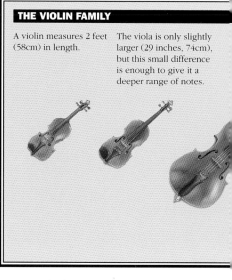

THE VIOLIN FAMILY

A violin measures 2 feet (58cm) in length.

The viola is only slightly larger (29 inches, 74cm), but this small difference is enough to give it a deeper range of notes.

Bow—made of wood and horsehair

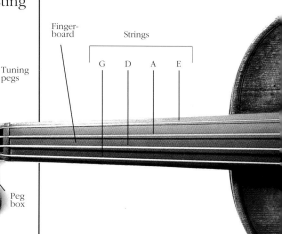

Scroll

Tuning pegs

Finger-board

Strings

G   D   A   E

Peg box

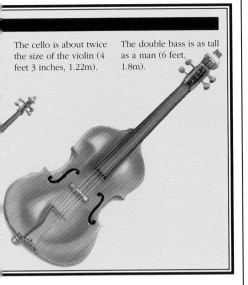

The cello is about twice the size of the violin (4 feet 3 inches, 1.22m).

The double bass is as tall as a man (6 feet, 1.8m).

How the strings are played

String instruments are played by plucking the strings or drawing a bow across them. This makes the strings vibrate and produce sound. The thicker, longer, and looser a string, the deeper the sound. The thinner, shorter, and tighter the string, the higher the sound. To produce different notes, the musician presses a string down with his finger to shorten it. The sound depends also on the instrument's size. A small violin produces much higher notes than a huge double bass. The frames, or resonators, of most stringed instruments are made from wood, which is ideal because it vibrates well. Some stringed instruments around the world also use gourds, the dried, hollowed-out husks of a large fruit, as resonators.

Violinists and viola players hold the bow with their right hand. They use their left hand to support the instrument and "stop" the strings.

Table

F-hole

Tailpiece

End pin

Waist

Bridge

DID YOU KNOW?

The Italian violin maker Antonio Stradivari (1644–1737) made over 1,000 instruments, including 540 violins. These are now considered the finest of all violins and are highly prized as masterpieces.

Deep and low

The cello, or violoncello, is a low-pitched, bass member of the string family. It is one of the most expressive of all instruments, and many pieces of orchestral music have been composed specifically for the cello, such as Sir Edward Elgar's *Cello Concerto*. The double bass is the deepest of all the string instruments. It is often played pizzicato (the strings are plucked), which produces a deep, resonant sound. It is played rhythmically in this way in jazz and folk music. Cellos and double basses are played in a vertical position, with the end pin resting on the floor. A cellist plays sitting down, and a double bass player sits on a high stool.

Other string instruments

Two solo instruments that have strings, but are not officially members of the string family, are the harp and the piano. A concert harp is nearly 6 feet (1.8m) high and has three pedals that change the pitch of the notes. A harpist plays with both hands, using the thumb and first three fingers. Several composers have included the gentle tones of the harp in their compositions, such as Holst's *The Planets* ("Venus").

DID YOU KNOW?

The piano was invented by an Italian, Bartolomeo Cristofori, in about 1701. He called the instrument the *pianoforte*—the "soft-loud."

Cellists support the neck of their instruments on their left shoulder and draw the bow across the strings with their right hand.

The piano

The solo piano was not included as an orchestral instrument until the beginning of this century. The strings of a concert grand piano are encased in a wooden frame with a keyboard attached. When notes are played, hammers strike the strings and bounce off again, allowing a wide range of soft and loud notes to be sounded.

The Woodwind Section

From the tiny piccolo to the booming bassoon, the instruments of the woodwind section produce a wide range of sounds and a contrasting tone to the strings.

Woodwind sounds

The woodwind section of an average orchestra consists of one piccolo, two flutes, two oboes, one cor anglais, two clarinets, one bass clarinet, two bassoons, and one double bassoon. They sit in the middle of the orchestra, behind the violas and in front of the brass and percussion sections. First developed in the 1700s and 1800s, woodwind instruments were then made entirely of wood, hence their name. Today they are made from wood and metal. Woodwind instruments are blown to produce sound. All wind instruments are also known as *aerophones*, which means they use air to sound different notes. Woodwind instruments such as the clarinet or flute often play solos.

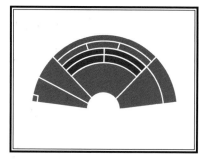

Double reed

Crook or bocal

Bell joint

Playing a woodwind instrument

A woodwind instrument is basically a long, hollow tube that you blow into or across. As you blow, the air inside the tube vibrates, producing sounds. To reach different notes, you cover or uncover the holes along the side of the tube. This makes the column (the air inside the tube) longer, to produce a lower note, or shorter, to produce a higher note. The sound also depends on the length and width of the individual instrument. The tiny piccolo makes a very high, rather shrill sound. The bassoon produces a deep, bass sound.

Mouthpieces

Most woodwind instruments, such as oboes and clarinets, have reeds (made of cane and fiberglass) in their mouthpieces. When you blow down into the mouthpiece, the reed vibrates and makes the air in the tube vibrate to produce sound. The oboe has a double reed, and these two reeds vibrate against each other to produce sound. A flute has a different type of mouthpiece. You hold the flute sideways and blow across a hole in its side to vibrate the air inside (there is more information about flutes on p. 23).

THE WOODWIND FAMILY

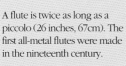

A flute is twice as long as a piccolo (26 inches, 67cm). The first all-metal flutes were made in the nineteenth century.

The oboe and clarinet are about the same size (25 inches, 64cm). The clarinet has a single reed; the oboe a double reed in its mouthpiece.

The mighty bassoon is 3 feet (88cm) long. Its size makes it a difficult instrument to play. The double bassoon is even bigger, and its sound is even lower.

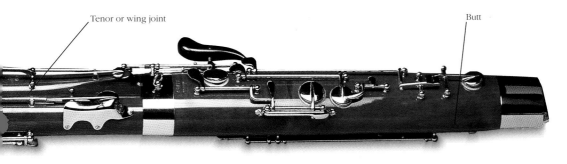

Tenor or wing joint

Butt

The origins of woodwind instruments

 oodwind instruments of all types have a long history, and many types are still used by people all over the world. The first flutes and whistles were made about 20,000 years ago from bear, bird, and deer bones, with holes pierced in them. Panpipes are another ancient type of flute, which are still played in South American music.

Mighty pipes

 mighty organ's pipes produce sound in the same way as a simple woodwind instrument, with a different pipe for each note. An organ also has several keyboards—usually two, but a grand organ may have as many as five keyboards. When an organ key is pressed, air is sent into different-sized pipes, creating high and low notes. The lowest notes in a large organ come from pipes almost 32 feet (10m) long. Some large concert halls have a concert organ, and several composers have added organ music to their orchestral works to create a majestic sound.

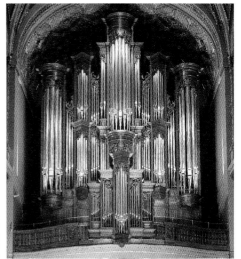

The organ in the Church of St. Ignatius Loyola in New York

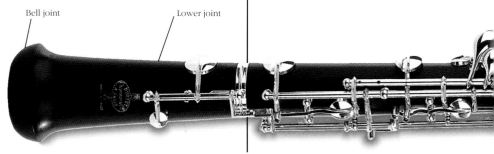

Bell joint   Lower joint

Pipes, piccolos, and flutes

imple pipes and flutes are held upright and are "end-blown" like a recorder. In some parts of the world, pipes are blown with the nose instead of the mouth. The panpipes are a set of pipes of different lengths, bound together and blown across the tops. They get their name from the ancient Greek myths of the god Pan, who used to play them. The type of flute played in modern orchestras, however, is the "side-blown" flute, often used in military bands in the United States and Britain. The piccolo is a small version of the flute and makes a bright, shrill sound, while the flute has a soft, breathy sound. Concert flutes are usually made from metal, but some are still made from wood to produce a softer tone. A flute player is called a flautist.

THE SAX

An instrument that developed from the woodwind family is the saxophone. It was invented by a Belgian, Adolphe Sax, in 1846, and it has a single-reed mouthpiece like a clarinet, with holes in the tube that are opened and closed by keys, levers, and pads, like other woodwind instruments. The saxophone is made of brass and was intended for military bands, but it became a popular jazz instrument. A few composers have written parts for it in their orchestral work, such as Bizet's incidental music for *L'Arlesienne*.

Flautists hold their instruments horizontally, with the mouthpiece held across the line of the lips.

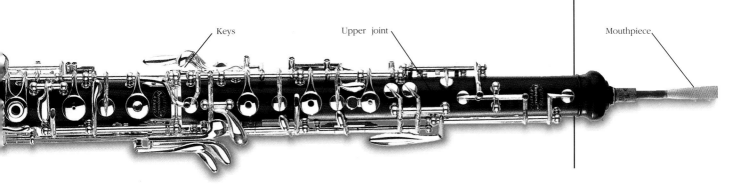

Keys   Upper joint   Mouthpiece

The Brass Section

The trumpets, trombones, horns, and tubas of the brass section provide a stirring contrast to the more delicate strings and woodwinds. They also are dramatic soloists, rising crisp and clear above the orchestra.

Fanfare of brass

For centuries, the piercing tones of trumpets and horns have been used to sound fanfares and battle and hunting calls, ringing out above the fray. In an orchestra, they produce a blaze of sound, adding a note of excitement and drama to any performance. The brass section of an average orchestra consists of four French horns, three trumpets, three trombones, and a tuba. They are positioned in the middle of the orchestra semicircle, sandwiched between the woodwind and percussion sections. Some composers have written music for a bigger brass section. Richard Wagner developed his version of the tuba, known as the Wagner tuba, for his series of operas, *The Ring of the Nibelung*.

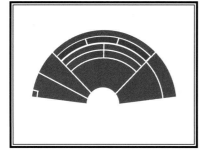

THE BRASS FAMILY

A trumpet measures 22 inches (56cm) in length.

A French horn is about the same length as a trumpet, but much bulkier and heavier. You need strong lips and lots of lung power to play one.

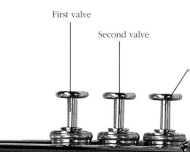

First valve

Second valve

Mouthpiece

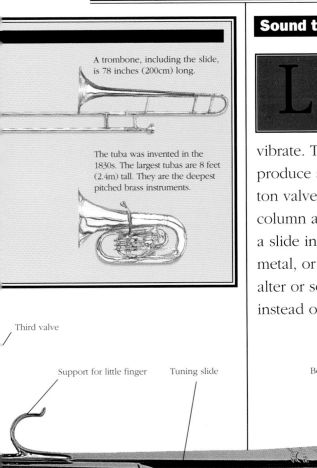

A trombone, including the slide, is 78 inches (200cm) long.

The tuba was invented in the 1830s. The largest tubas are 8 feet (2.4m) tall. They are the deepest pitched brass instruments.

Sound the trumpets

Like the woodwind family, brass instruments use air to produce sound. To play a brass instrument, you purse your lips against the mouthpiece and blow hard into it, making your lips vibrate. These vibrations travel down into the instrument to produce a sound. To play different notes, you press the piston valves down; this adds to or cuts off sections of the air column and changes the sound. (A trombone player moves a slide in and out instead.) You can also insert a plug of wood, metal, or plastic, called a *mute*, into the end of the instrument to alter or soften the sound. Horn players sometimes use their hand, instead of a mute, to change the tone.

Trumpet players sit upright so that they can control their breathing.

Third valve

Support for little finger   Tuning slide

Bell—helps throw sound outward

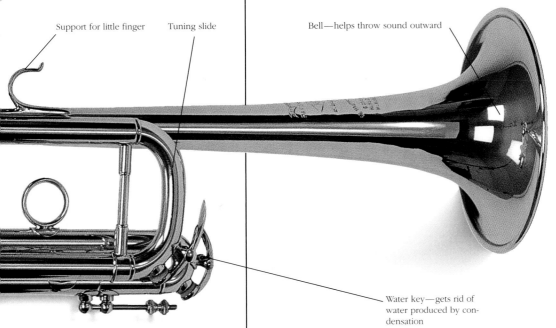

Water key—gets rid of water produced by condensation

DID YOU KNOW?

A type of trumpet was found in the tomb of the Egyptian pharaoh, Tutankhamun. It is over 3,000 years old.

The serpent was a very odd instrument, invented in France in 1590. A cross between woodwind and brass, its name came from its twisting, snakelike coils. The tuba has now replaced it.

A blast of brass

T he first horns were made from hollowed-out branches and animal horns. Brass horns were used to sound out hunting signals as long ago as the fourteenth century. In Haydn and Mozart's time, the trumpet was used to add strength to the orchestral sound. However, trumpets then were still *natural*, meaning without valves, so they could only produce a few different notes. The three-valve trumpet was developed in the nineteenth century. It could play all the notes of the scale. The French horn was developed from an early French hunting horn. It is two horns in one: the player's thumb works a valve that switches between two sets of coiled tubes, thus varying the pitch of the notes.

SLIDING SCALE

Trombones date back to the fifteenth century when new skills in metalwork brought improvements to all brass instruments. Beethoven was one of the first composers to include trombones in the classical orchestra, in *Symphony No. 5*, but not until the nineteenth century did trombones became regular members of the brass section.

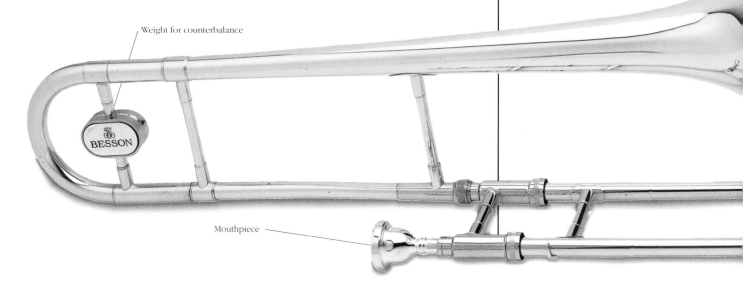

Weight for counterbalance

BESSON

Mouthpiece

Bring on the band

Brass instruments are ideal for military bands because they can be easily carried in parades. The American bandmaster John Philip Sousa designed a large, deep-sounding brass instrument called a sousaphone. It twists around the player's shoulders with the bell raised high above the head, so it is ideal for playing in a marching band. Brass bands play in many different countries and include instruments such as cornets,

flügelhorns, and euphoniums. Early British brass bands have existed for more than 150 years, and some British composers, such as Sir Edward Elgar and Ralph Vaughan Williams, have written music for brass bands.

A military brass band

Bell

Slide

Water key

The Percussion Section

From the crash of cymbals and the beat of drums, to the shaking and rattling of bells and maracas, the percussion section is the special effects department of the orchestra.

Shake, rattle, and roll

 he percussion section completes the orchestra. It is the loudest group of instruments, positioned right at the back behind the brass section. It is also the most varied group, including timpani (kettledrums), bass and side drums, tubular bells, xylophones, glockenspiels, cymbals, and triangles, together with hand bells, wood blocks, gongs, and rattles. Many percussion instruments were added to orchestras in the nineteenth century, to produce a greater range of special musical effects.

Beating drums

 ost percussion instruments are struck in some way, with a stick or hands. When you hit a drum, the membrane, or skin, stretched over the drum's frame vibrates and sets the air inside the drum vibrating too. This produces sound. The tighter the membrane, the faster it vibrates when struck and the higher the note produced. Larger frames produce deeper notes than smaller ones, so the bigger the drum, the louder and deeper the sound.

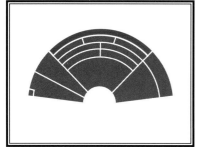

THE PERCUSSION FAMILY

An orchestra may have as many as six timpani, or kettledrums, beating out the rhythm or playing a drumroll.

Shell—main body or frame of drum

Struts for support

Pedal—used to change note by altering the tightness of the drumhead

Gongs and cymbals can produce great crashing sounds.

Each of the xylophone's wooden bars produces a different note.

Pitched and unpitched

P ercussion instruments are divided into two groups— pitched and unpitched. Pitched instruments, such as xylophones and bells, produce definite musical notes when played. Unpitched instruments, such as tambourines, maracas, and cymbals, simply produce a soft or loud noise. The large timpani or kettledrum can be made to sound different notes by tightening the skin or drumhead. The timpanist can also use the pedal to change the note while playing.

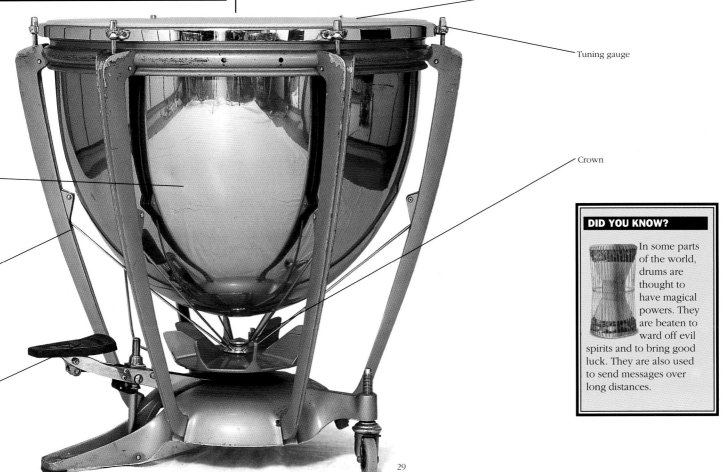

Drumhead—the membrane or skin

Tuning gauge

Crown

DID YOU KNOW?

In some parts of the world, drums are thought to have magical powers. They are beaten to ward off evil spirits and to bring good luck. They are also used to send messages over long distances.

Unusual sounds

Sometimes more unusual percussion instruments are needed in an orchestra. A wind machine is a kind of revolving barrel inside a tight canvas cover. When the handle is turned it creates the sound of wind, and the pitch gets higher as the handle is turned faster.

Tubular bells are metal tubes of different length suspended from a frame that are struck with hammers. They can be heard in Debussy's *Ibéria*, the second of his three orchestral *Images*.

The tambourine is really a small drum with metal jingles fitted into a wooden frame. It is most commonly associated with Spanish or gypsy music. In Stravinsky's ballet *Petrushka,* a tambourine is dropped on the floor to signal the death of the heroine.

(left)
The percussion section of an orchestra

(right)
Percussion players in action

Ancient origins

Drums and bells are probably the oldest of all instruments. In Africa and China, drums were being used thousands of years ago to send messages.

Traditionally, the West Indian steel drum is made from an oil drum. Instead of a skin, one end of the drum is beaten down and divided into segments, each of which produces a different note. There are six sizes of steel drum—the rhythm drum, the ping pong, the double second, guitar, cello, and bass.

West Indian steel drums

ROCK 'N' ROLL

Percussion instruments are played with incredible energy and coordination by the drummer of a rock band or jazz group. The drummer sits at a drum kit to play a variety of drums and cymbals, using the hands and feet. Several instruments in a drum kit, such as the snare and bass drums, are also used by the percussionist in an orchestra.

Music for Orchestras

Orchestration is the art of writing music specifically for an orchestra and its particular blend of instruments. This has produced some of the greatest works of classical music, including many famous symphonies.

Early music

At first, orchestras played music written to accompany ballets and operas. But in the early eighteenth century, composers such as Bach and Handel began writing pieces for orchestra alone. These pieces were called *concerti grossi*, or great concertos. They were written mainly for strings, contrasting a large group of players with a smaller group or a soloist.

A painting of eighteenth-century musicans

CHAMBER MUSIC

Originally written to be performed in private houses, chamber music is played by small groups of two or more instruments. Early chamber music was written for two violins, a cello, and a harpsichord, but the most well-known combination is the string quartet, which was developed in the early eighteenth century. Schubert wrote several quintets, for four strings and a piano, and Mendelssohn even wrote octets.

The age of the symphony

In the mid-eighteenth century, composers began to write longer pieces, called symphonies, for larger orchestras. Symphony orchestras take their name from this type of music. A symphony is made up of three or four separate sections, called movements. Franz Joseph Haydn (1732–1809), who wrote over 100 symphonies, preferred four movements—a lively opening, a slow movement, a dancelike movement, and an exciting finale. In the nineteenth century, a new type of orchestral music that painted a picture or told a story became very popular. It was called *programme music* after the notes written for the audience by composers to explain what their music was about.

Settling the score

Orchestral music written on paper is called a score. It shows the parts to be played by each instrument or family. The system of signs and symbols used to write music down today dates from the twelfth century. It was devised by monks to help them record different ways of singing hymns and psalms. Modern orchestral scores are usually printed in a book. The woodwind parts are arranged at the top of the page and the strings at the bottom.

MUSICAL TERMS

Composers write instructions on the score to tell the orchestra how to play it. Most of the terms used are written in Italian because music was first printed in Italy.

Tempo words:
Adagio—fairly slow.
Allegro—fast, lively.
Andante—steadily, at a leisurely pace.
Largo—slow and stately.
Rallentando—slowing down gradually.

Mood words:
Appassionato—with passion, verve.
Lacrimoso—sadly, tearfully.
Legato—smoothly.
Maestoso—majestically, regally.
Staccato—briskly, each note at a time.

Volume words:
Crescendo—get louder.
Diminuendo—get quieter.
Forte—loud.
Mezzo forte—quite loud.
Pianissimo—very quiet.

A detail from a handwritten score of music by Bach

Choral music

The earliest choral music was performed by monks. By the seventeenth century, composers found a way to combine choral music with orchestral accompaniment in an oratorio. Handel developed this kind of sung religious storytelling in his dramatic work the *Messiah*. Other well-known oratorios are Haydn's *The Creation* and Mendelssohn's *Elijah*. Another type of choral music for choir and orchestra is the requiem, a Catholic Mass for the dead. Benjamin Britten wrote his *War Requiem* as a memorial to the Second World War; it combines the Latin words of the Mass with the war poems of Wilfred Owen.

Benjamin Britten rehearsing his **War Requiem** *in Coventry Cathedral*

BALLET

Ballet, like opera, tells a story with music but the dancers use actions instead of words. Tchaikovsky composed the music for some of the most famous ballets ever written— *Sleeping Beauty*, *Swan Lake*, and *The Nutcracker*. More recently, the modern American composer Aaron Copland (1900–1990) wrote ballets such as *Billy the Kid* and *Rodeo* for a more modern style of dance.

DID YOU KNOW?

King George III was so moved when he first heard the "Hallelujah" chorus from Handel's *Messiah* that he made the audience stand up. This practice is still followed today.

Opera

Opera began in the sixteenth century in Italy. Early operas were based on ancient Greek legends and were performed in the new public opera houses (the first opened in Venice in 1637). By the eighteenth century, opera had become a popular form of entertainment throughout Europe, and opera singers were as famous as modern-day film stars. Many of Mozart's operas, such as *The Marriage of Figaro*, are amusing, while other operas tell tragic stories, such as Bizet's *Carmen*. Today, great opera singers like Pavarotti and Jessye Norman make opera popular around the world.

MUSICALS

These modern-day, lighter versions of opera tell a story with spoken words, like a play, as well as catchy songs included throughout the performance. The American writers Richard Rodgers and Oscar Hammerstein produced many famous musicals in the 1940s and 1950s, including *Oklahoma!* and *Carousel*, and today Andrew Lloyd Webber's musicals continue to fill theaters on Broadway and in London's West End.

(left) A scene from **Carmen** *by Bizet*

(right) A scene from **The Magic Flute** *by Mozart*

Famous Composers

Many of the world's greatest composers have written for the orchestra. Most were gifted musicians in their own right, often playing in or conducting their own works. Their music may be centuries old, but it is still played today by orchestras all over the world.

Composing for kings

I n the baroque period, composers were employed by the king, the aristocracy, or by the Church. They had to write music for church services, private court performances, and such royal occasions as coronations and weddings. Two of the greatest baroque composers were Bach and Handel.

DID YOU KNOW?

Handel was born in the same year as Bach, and in the same country, but he outlived him by nine years. He spent most of his life in London where he composed music for the English royal family. Among his most famous works are *Water Music* and *Music for the Royal Fireworks*, both specially written for royal occasions. Handel also wrote many famous choral works, including the *Messiah* and several anthems for the coronation of King George II.

Johann Sebastian Bach (1685–1750) Bach was born in Eisenach, Germany, into a large musical family. In his lifetime he won great fame as a brilliant organist but not as a composer. His own work was only really appreciated after his death. While employed at the court of Prince Leopold of Anhalt-Cöthen, Bach wrote some of his greatest orchestral works.

A fireworks display on the Thames, London, which would have been accompanied by Handel's **Music for the Royal Fireworks**

Classical composers

Two of the most brilliant and prolific classical composers were Mozart and Haydn. Most composers at this time still relied on the support of wealthy sponsors, although Mozart had to make his living by giving public concerts.

Wolfgang Amadeus Mozart
(1756–1791)

Mozart began composing when he was just four years old and wrote his first sonata at the age of five. As a child, he toured all over Europe, giving concerts to show off his genius. As a rebellious adult, however, Mozart was difficult to employ. Despite an enormous output of work, he was often poverty-stricken and died a few weeks before his thirty-sixth birthday. Among Mozart's most famous works are forty-one symphonies and several operas, including *Don Giovanni*, *The Magic Flute*, and *The Marriage of Figaro*. Sadly, Mozart died before he finished his *Requiem*.

Franz-Joseph Haydn
(1732–1809)

Haydn began his musical career as a chorister in Vienna, Austria, but spent most of his working life as the court composer to the Hungarian Esterházy family. He composed music at an extraordinary rate, and his fame soon spread throughout Europe. Haydn wrote more than 100 symphonies, including "The Military," "The Clock," and "The Surprise" symphonies. His best-known choral work, *The Creation*, was inspired by the music of Handel. Haydn retired from his work for the Esterházys after 40 years' service. He attended a special performance of *The Creation* to celebrate his seventy-sixth birthday, the year before he died.

DID YOU KNOW?

In his short life, Mozart wrote some 1,000 symphonies, sonatas, operas, concertos, serenades, and other pieces of religious or chamber music. Only seventy of these were published in his lifetime. He is said to have written three symphonies in just forty-two days and a whole opera (*La Clemenza di Tito*) in just 18 days.

The Bach family contained at least seventy-six musicians, of whom Johann Sebastian was the most gifted. More than fifty of the Bachs had the same first name—Johann!

By the age of five, Handel could play the harpsichord, organ, violin, and oboe.

CLASSICS

Other classical composers include

Clementi (1752–1832)

Field (1782–1837)

Schubert (1797–1828)

Bring on the romantics

By the romantic period, composers no longer had to depend on wealthy patrons to employ and pay them. With the rise of concert halls and professional orchestras, they were now able to make a living from public performances of their music. Beethoven and Tchaikovsky were two of the greatest composers of this time.

Ludwig van Beethoven
(1770–1827)

Beethoven was born in Bonn, Germany, but spent most of his life in Vienna, Austria. By the age of thirty, he had established a reputation as a brilliant pianist who also sometimes composed. But by 1800 Beethoven's hearing had begun to fail, and for the last ten years of his life he was completely deaf. Amazingly, this was when he composed some of the world's greatest orchestral music, including his famous nine symphonies. *Symphony No. 9* (the "Choral") was the first symphony ever to include human voices. In his final years, Beethoven wrote several beautiful string quartets. He was recognized as a great musical genius in his lifetime.

Peter Ilyich Tchaikovsky
(1840–1893)

The Russian composer Tchaikovsky grew up in St. Petersburg, where his father was a government official. He was supposed to train for a career in law but he soon discovered he was more interested in music. He is best known for his symphonies, including the famous *1812 Overture*, which tells the story of Napoleon's retreat from Moscow, and his ballet scores, such as *Swan Lake, Sleeping Beauty,* and *The Nutcracker*. Despite the great musical success he enjoyed, Tchaikovsky had a deeply unhappy personal life. It is believed that he committed suicide by drinking poison at the age of fifty-three.

DID YOU KNOW?

As a penniless young classical composer, Franz Schubert (1797–1828) wrote as many as eight songs a day. He always slept with his glasses on in case an idea for a song came to him and he needed to write it down quickly.

ROMANTICS

Other romantic composers include

Mendelssohn (1809–1847)

Berlioz (1803–1869)

Chopin (1810–1849)

Liszt (1811–1886)

Brahms (1833–1897)

Verdi (1813–1901)

Wagner (1813–1883)

Composition in the twentieth century

Gustav Mahler

(1860–1911)

The German composer Gustav Mahler supported himself through his early musical career by giving piano lessons. As his reputation grew, he was able to earn his living conducting operas. He composed his own music when the opera houses closed for the summer. Mahler wrote nine symphonies and many songs. His music is very moody and atmospheric, full of drama and passion.

Benjamin Britten

(1913–1976)

The English composer Benjamin Britten became famous in 1945 with the performance of his opera *Peter Grimes*, and three years later founded his own opera company. Britten wrote many different types of music, from operas to concertos, symphonies to sonatas. He used traditional ideas put together in new and unexpected ways. He wrote the music for *The Young Person's Guide to the Orchestra* in 1946, to introduce the instruments of the orchestra to young people.

Aaron Copland (1900–1990)

The American composer with Russian Jewish parents was born in New York but studied in Paris. He is probably most famous for his three "cowboy ballets"—*Billy the Kid, Rodeo,* and *Appalachian Spring*. He also wrote a symphony for the organ.

Benjamin Britten

Great Orchestras

Today most major cities in the world have their own symphony orchestras. Many of these date from the nineteenth century when professional orchestras were established and led by famous conductors all over Europe and the United States.

The Mannheim Orchestra

The first modern symphony orchestra was founded in 1743 in the German city of Mannheim. Funded by the Duke of Mannheim, this court orchestra was packed with the best, most skillful musicians of the day. The orchestra had such a good reputation that many famous composers, including Mozart, wrote music expressly for it. The size of the Mannheim Orchestra, which consisted of twenty violins, four violas, four cellos and double basses, two flutes, two oboes, two bassoons, and two timpani, four horns and a trumpet, became the standard orchestral group at that time.

Cloth Hall concerts

The oldest symphony orchestra still playing is the Leipzig Gewandhaus Orchestra. *Gewandhaus* is the German word for *cloth makers hall*. It refers to the concert hall built just for the orchestra by the city's linen merchants. This was one of the first concert halls.

Sir Edward Elgar recording with the London Philharmonic Orchestra

1881 The Boston Symphony Orchestra is founded in the United States

1882 The Amsterdam Concertegbouw Orchestra and the Berlin Philharmonic are founded

1891 Founding of the Chicago Philharmonic in the United States

1901 The Czech Philharmonic becomes an independent orchestra (formerly the orchestra of Prague National Opera)

1901 The Warsaw Philharmonic is founded in Poland

1904 Formation of the London Symphony Orchestra (LSO)

1932 Formation of the London Philharmonic Orchestra

Orchestras in America

The oldest symphony orchestra in the United States, the New York Philharmonic, gave its first concert in December 1842. Most American cities now have at least one outstanding symphony orchestra, and many of these travel all over the world to give concerts as well as perform in their own cities' concert halls.

London listening

Two of the world's finest orchestras are based in London, England. The London Symphony Orchestra was formed in 1904. It gives about eighty concerts a year, as well as recording and touring. The composer Edward Elgar (1857–1934) was one of its early conductors. The London Philharmonic Orchestra was formed in 1932. In 1956, it became the first British orchestra to tour Russia.

DID YOU KNOW?

The Boston Symphony Orchestra is world famous for its Boston Pops, a series of lighthearted concerts first performed in 1885. Arthur Fiedler became conductor of the Boston Pops in 1930 and made them internationally renowned through numerous recordings.

The Austrian conductor Herbert von Karajan (1908 – 1989) was one of the most respected conductors of all time. For thirty-five years, he was principal conductor of the Berlin Philharmonic. He also conducted the London Philharmonic and the Vienna State Opera and made over 800 recordings of major orchestral works.

The New York Philharmonic Orchestra with conductor Kurt Masur

Orchestras of the World

The symphony orchestra originated in Europe and largely plays Western classical music. But groups of musicians have also played together for thousands of years in other parts of the world.

The gamelan sound

The gamelan is a type of orchestra found in Indonesia. The main instruments are percussion instruments, including gongs, chimes, drums, and xylophones, with some string and woodwind instruments. There may be as many as twenty to forty musicians. Each town or village has its own local gamelan. It often accompanies traditional dancing or shadow play performances. The musicians memorize their music, then improvise around certain set melodies.

DID YOU KNOW?

One Indian court musician in the sixteenth century was said to be such a genius that he could make night fall by singing the appropriate raga.

_____

An ancient Greek orchestra might have contained a lyre, a harp, panpipes, cymbals, a *timpanon* (like a tambourine), and an *auloi* (set of double pipes). We don't know how Greek music sounded because it was not written down.

A gamelan orchestra

Indian classical music

A classical Indian group might consist of a sitar (a stringed instrument played like a guitar), *tablas* (drums), and a *sarangi* (a stringed instrument played with a bow, like a cello), or a *shahnai* (a woodwind instrument, like an oboe). The musicians do not play from a fixed score but improvise around patterns of notes, called ragas. There are hundreds of ragas designed for different times of the day and to create different moods. A raga is made up of five to seven notes, played in ascending or descending order.

South American music

Flutes and pipes such as panpipes are often played in South American music, giving a soft, dreamy sound. More unusual stringed instruments, like the harp pictured below, are played by some South American Indians, such as these Quecha Indians. Mariachi bands, consisting of violins, guitars, trumpets, and a singer, are common in Mexico.

BANDS

Bands are smaller than orchestras and are often made up of one type of instrument, such as percussion or brass. Brass bands, military bands, folk bands, even one-man bands are found all over the world. Traditional jazz bands contain brass and woodwind instruments, with a piano and a rhythmic double bass.

(left)
South American Quecha Indian players

(right)
Jazz trumpeter Wynton Marsalis

Instruments of the World

Musical instruments have developed all over the world to suit different cultures. Many modern orchestral instruments have their roots in the Middle East and Asia.

National instruments

The sound of certain instruments reminds us of a particular country. The clicking of castanets conjures up a picture of whirling Spanish dancers, and the twang of the sitar is unmistakably Indian. Ancient tribes from different parts of the world made instruments with their own unique sound. These could be used to send messages to other members of the tribe, rather like an early telephone system.

Musicians from the Amazon playing Urena flutes

INSTRUMENTS OF THE WORLD

Balalaika—a Russian instrument, like a guitar with a triangular body and three strings.

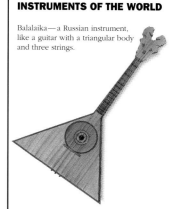

Koto—a Japanese instrument, made from a long box with thirteen strings stretched along it. It is played on the ground by plucking the strings.

DID YOU KNOW?

The *charango* is a small South American lute that traditionally was made from armadillo skin. The armadillo is now a protected animal so the instrument makers have to use wood instead.

Bagpipes have existed for more than 3,000 years. They are still a popular instrument in the Scottish Highlands of Britain. The piper blows into the mouth pipe called the chanter to inflate the bag, which is then squeezed to sound the other pipes called the drones.

Where in the world?

The map below shows where many different instruments come from. Although they all look quite different, they are only variations of the four families: string, woodwind, brass, and percussion. These national instruments are still handcrafted in their native countries.

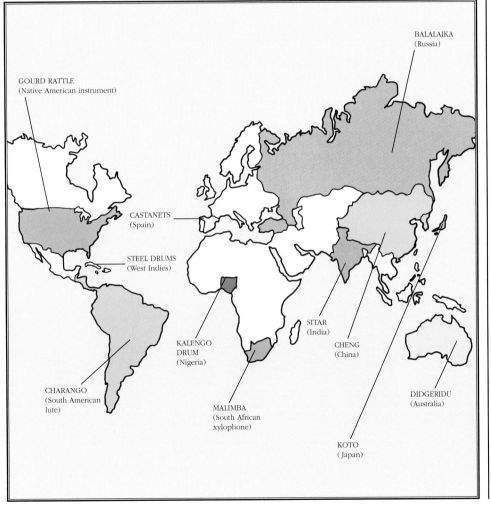

GOURD RATTLE
(Native American instrument)

BALALAIKA
(Russia)

CASTANETS
(Spain)

STEEL DRUMS
(West Indies)

SITAR
(India)

CHENG
(China)

KALENGO
DRUM
(Nigeria)

CHARANGO
(South American
lute)

MALIMBA
(South African
xylophone)

DIDGERIDU
(Australia)

KOTO
(Japan)

INSTRUMENTS OF THE WORLD

Panpipes—a set of whistlelike flutes, bound together in order of size. Each pipe produces a single note when you blow across the top. An important instrument in South American music.

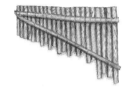

Castanets—Spanish instruments, made from two small hollowed-out pieces of wood, clacked together. Used to accompany flamenco dancing.

Kalengo drum—a double-headed drum from Nigeria, used to beat out the sounds of an African language.

Didgeridu—a traditional Aborigine instrument from Australia. Made from a hollow eucalyptus branch, blown at one end.

Playing in an Orchestra

Now that you know all about the instruments and history of the orchestra, it is time to look at the musicians. What does it take to be a professional musician? Musical ability, nerves of steel, dedication—and much more!

Learning an instrument

The first step to becoming a good musician is to learn to play an instrument well. This means having regular lessons and taking music exams to demonstrate technical ability. It may be possible to borrow an instrument from your school or college to start with, as some instruments are expensive.

Young musicians at an audition

CHILD'S PLAY

Several composers have written music just for children. You can listen to *The Young Person's Guide to the Orchestra* by Benjamin Britten on the CD at the front of this book. In Prokofiev's musical story of *Peter and the Wolf* and Saint-Saëns' *Carnival of the Animals*, the composers have used a different orchestral instrument to represent each animal.

DID YOU KNOW?

Some children become gifted musicians at a very young age. Mozart could play the piano by the age of three and was composing by the time he was five. Chopin was a concert pianist by the time he was seven, and Prokofiev had written two operas by the age of eleven.

Joining an orchestra

You may be able to have lessons at school or you can ask your music teacher to suggest a local teacher for your instrument. He or she will teach you to play, to read music, and to improve your technique. As soon as you feel ready, try to get some experience by playing in a school or youth orchestra. This will help you get used to being part of a team and performing in front of an audience. If you are good enough to join a professional orchestra, you will have to attend an audition where you play for and talk to the conductor and some of the senior players. Some musicians study at music college before joining an orchestra. Whichever path you choose, don't forget to play every day. Even the world's greatest musicians have to keep practicing!

A school orchestra in concert

Running an Orchestra

A huge amount of time and money is needed to keep a symphony orchestra running. Many orchestras are managed by a board of directors, or a committee that appoints the principal conductor. A general manager looks after daily affairs.

Rehearsals

An orchestra spends much of its time rehearsing. This enables the musicians to learn the music and to get an idea of how the conductor wants them to play it. The conductor goes through the score piece by piece, rehearsing each group of instruments separately and then together. The conductor may go over difficult sections again and again until they are just right.

Sir Colin Davis, principal conductor, rehearsing with the London Symphony Orchestra

CD COLLECTION

There are hundreds of recordings of the same pieces of classical music. None of them sounds the same because they are played by different orchestras and interpreted by different conductors.

Recording

Orchestras make recordings of famous classical works and music written for films or television. This type of music is called a soundtrack and it is recorded in a sound-proof recording studio. In the early days of silent films, an orchestra played excerpts from famous works to fit the action on the screen. Today the film director chooses a composer to write an original soundtrack that suits the subject and mood of the film. Recordings are one way that the orchestra earns its income. It also receives money from ticket sales for concerts, and larger sums come from government grants or special art foundation grants.

The London Symphony Orchestra in a recording studio

Life in an orchestra

Life in a professional orchestra is hectic and demanding but extremely exciting. The musicians cannot afford to take things for granted, though, as there are always plenty of others waiting to take their place if they do not work hard and perform well. Not only does the orchestra perform concerts, it tours nationally and abroad. Transporting a whole symphony orchestra—musicians, instruments, music, and all—is a mighty task.

About *The Young Person's Guide to the Orchestra*

 Benjamin Britten was asked to write *The Young Person's Guide to the Orchestra* in 1945 for an educational film about the different instruments of the symphony orchestra. The most recent recordings of the music are now available on cassette and CD with a narrator's voice explaining the sounds of each instrument.

The music begins with an introduction to the four groups, or families, of orchestral instruments presented in this book: the strings, the woodwinds, the brass, and the percussion. Britten then illustrates the sounds of the different groups in a set of thirteen variations on a piece of orchestral music by Henry Purcell, a composer Britten greatly admired. Each variation highlights the characteristics of particular instruments: the flute plays breathy gentle notes with its shrill little brother the piccolo, the cellos and double basses make deep, rich sounds, while the brass and percussion instruments play loud triumphant music. Once all the instruments have played individually, Britten brings them together, one by one, in a fugue that builds into a dramatic piece of music for the whole orchestra. In an exciting finale the brass section plays music by Purcell, called "Fine Melody," while the other instruments play Britten's fugue.

The Young Person's Guide to the Orchestra is one of the best known of Britten's orchestral works. It is far more than a guide to the instruments—in fact, today it is considered an original and inventive piece of music in its own right. It is listened to, and played by, children and adults in concert halls; and there are many different recordings of this piece from around the world.

Benjamin Britten

Benjamin Britten was born in 1913 in Suffolk, on the east coast of England. He began composing at the age of five and had written a string quartet by the time he was ten. He studied at The Royal College of Music in London, England, where he also became a skilled pianist. His first major opera, *Peter Grimes*, tells the story of a simple fisherman and reflects his love for his seaside home.

Britten spent several years working in America, as well as visiting Russia and the Far East. In Bali, he was so impressed with the gamelan orchestras that he included some of their effects in his final opera, *Death in Venice*. He was a strong pacifist and visited many British hospitals and bomb sites during the Second World War, giving concerts for the injured and homeless. In 1962 he wrote his famous *War Requiem* for the consecration of the new Coventry Cathedral, which was rebuilt after the original was bombed during the war. This magnificent choral work combines the Latin words of the requiem Mass with war poems by the British poet Wilfred Owen.

As well as writing many operas and choral works, folk songs, and music for film, Britten composed several pieces of music for non-professional musicians, such as *Let's Make an Opera, Saint Nicholas*, and, of course, *The Young Person's Guide to the Orchestra*. Throughout his life, he enjoyed working with musicians of all standards, and especially children. He is considered one of the greatest composers of the twentieth century.

Index

Glossary

ballet   A theatrical representation of a story or a theme performed to music by ballet dancers.

baroque   The musical movement that lasted from 1600–1750. The name is derived from the grand, ornate style of architecture popular at that time.

chamber music   Music written for and played by a small group of music instrumentalists.

classical   The musical movement that lasted from about 1750–1825. In music, as well as architecture, it described a style that was more graceful than the baroque style.

concerto grosso   (Italian for *great concerts.*) A composition in which a small group of solo instruments is contrasted with the main orchestra. This type of concert was very popular in the baroque period.

gamelan   A group of musicians who play mainly percussion instruments, found in Indonesia.

hymns   Christian religious songs of praise.

movement   A self-contained section of a large composition, usually having its own structure and tempo.

mute   A plug of wood or metal that can be inserted into the end of an instrument to alter or soften the sound.

notation   Any series of symbols to write down music.

octet   A composition for eight voices or instruments.

opera   A play set to music, for singers and an orchestra.

oratorio   A musical composition for soloists, chorus, and orchestra, usually based on a religious theme and performed in a church or concert hall.

orchestra   A group of musicians who play a variety of instruments grouped into four families: strings, woodwind, brass, and percussion.

overture   A piece of orchestral music played at the beginning of an opera, ballet, or musical.

pianola   A mechanical piano; the keys are controlled by air which is supplied through small holes in a moving paper roll.

pitch   The highness or lowness of a musical note, which is measured by the frequency of its vibrations.

pizzicato   (Italian for *pinched.*) Instruction to pluck the strings of normally bowed instruments.

psalms   Religious sung verses from the Old Testament of the Bible.

quintet   A group of five singers or instrumentalists or a piece of music composed for such a group.

raga   Any of the many patterns of melody and rhythm in Indian music that create different moods.

requiem   A Catholic Mass for the dead; any piece of music composed or performed as a memorial to the dead.

romantic   The musical movement that was popular in the 19th century. As its name suggests, the romantic style of music was expressive and emotional.

score   A written piece of music showing how all the vocal and instrumental parts should be played.

sonata   An extended composition in several movements written for one (e.g., piano sonata) or more instruments.

string quartet   An instrumental group consisting of two violins, one viola, and one cello.

symphony   An extended large-scale orchestral composition, usually with several movements.

viol   The forerunner to the violin. It had six strings, a flat back and was held between the knees and played with a curved bow.

Acknowledgments

The publishers would like to thank all those who supplied photographs for this book,
particularly the London Symphony Orchestra and Keith Saunders.
The copyright owners are listed below:

Keith Saunders: pp. 8, 15, 28/29, 46, 47, 48 left, 49
Range/Bettmann/UPI: p. 9
Bridgeman Art Library/Conservatory of St Peter, Naples/Giraudon: p. 10 top
Bridgeman Art Library/Louvre, Paris/Giraudon: p. 10 bottom (painting by Limousin)
Bridgeman Art Library/Louvre, Paris/Giraudon: p. 12 (painting by Pannini)
Bridgeman Art Library: pp. 32, 36 right
Hulton Deutsch: pp. 13, 17 bottom, 33, 34, 36 left, 37, 38, 39, 41
Royal Philharmonic Orchestra: p. 14
Morris and Smith Ltd.: p. 16/17 (violin) and jacket
Frederick Phelps Ltd.: p. 16/17 (violin bow)
Phil Starling: pp. 17 top, 18 top, 23 top, 25, 26
Salvi International Ltd.: p. 18 bottom
BZ Advertising: p. 19
Phillips: p. 20/21
Boosey and Hawkes: pp. 22/23, 23 right, 24/25, 26/27
N.P. Mander Ltd.: p. 22
The Military Picture Library: p. 27
Redferns Picture Library: p. 30
The Hutchison Library: pp. 31, 42, 43, 44
Dominic Photography (Catherine Ashmore): p. 35
The New York Philharmonic Orchestra: p. 40/41
Polygram: p. 48 right